Living with Changes

Poetic Reflections for a Good Life

Astrid Hardjana-Large

BALBOA.
PRESS
A DIVISION OF HAY HOUSE

Balboa Press books may be ordered through booksellers or by contacting:

Balboa Press
A Division of Hay House
1663 Liberty Drive
Bloomington, IN 47403
www.balboapress.com
1 (877) 407-4847

Because of the dynamic nature of the Internet, any web addresses or
links contained in this book may have changed since publication and
may no longer be valid. The views expressed in this work are solely those
of the author and do not necessarily reflect the views of the publisher,
and the publisher hereby disclaims any responsibility for them.

The author of this book does not dispense medical advice or prescribe the use
of any technique as a form of treatment for physical, emotional, or medical
problems without the advice of a physician, either directly or indirectly. The
intent of the author is only to offer information of a general nature to help you
in your quest for emotional and spiritual well-being. In the event you use any
of the information in this book for yourself, which is your constitutional right,
the author and the publisher assume no responsibility for your actions.

Any people depicted in stock imagery provided by Thinkstock are models,
and such images are being used for illustrative purposes only.
Certain stock imagery © Thinkstock.

Printed in the United States of America.

ISBN: 978-1-4525-9741-6 (sc)
ISBN: 978-1-4525-9742-3 (e)

Balboa Press rev. date: 11/5/2014

Dedication to: Theresa Hardjana, Chadwick
Large and Caitlin Large, people who have inspired
me to keep on trying and never give up.

Contents

Introduction

Welcome to my collection of poetry. This collection is a reflection of experiences since Epilepsy became a part of my life. It has been my goal to accept Epilepsy into my life and with this goal I have been blessed with life lessons. It is my desire to share and encourage others to never give up. It can take a lot of work to not allow your health to take you over but the gifts received are valuable rewards.

It is my desire to be an inspiration to all my readers. Please enjoy my work.

Changes

My Epilepsy

As frustrating as it can be
I have to accept that it is a part of me
Wherever I may want to go
It is something that will show
My Epilepsy

I have often tried to deny
I have often needed to rely
Help is a word I use
Help is something I cannot refuse
To me, many cautions apply

This is not the end of my life
It is something to live with, a strife
I will still be able to succeed
As long as I choose to proceed
Epilepsy, not the center of my life

These are words written when life was looked upon to accept having Epilepsy. As frustrating as Epilepsy is acceptance that it is a part your person is important. There are times when seizures are silent and people don't know about them, but it has to be admitted that having Epilepsy will still show.

As a person works to accept they may wish to deny its existence. They want to be a person without worries but it has to be admitted that they need others. Help is a word that one uses due to the preventions epilepsy can create. When others offer help, it is not wise to refuse it. When a person with epilepsy goes out into the world they have to plan their journey, many cautions apply to that person. Acceptance of epilepsy into life; a person is not allowing their life to end. It is something that they live with. It can appear as a hardship but it is not an end. It is up to each person to choose what they want and to work towards their goals. Epilepsy is not a focus for one's life; it is a part of that person but not defining them. People with epilepsy may still succeed as long as they proceed.

Changes Are Not My Fault

Apologies to the self
For the things I cannot control
Looking for good reason
As to why it has a role

A confusion to others
In my shakes and falls
A frustration to me
As it changes and appalls

I have to accept
I cannot have my wanted ways
I have to always be ready
For changes in any day

Changes are not my fault
It's time for me to realize
Stop feeling guilt or shame
No need to continuously apologize

This is a reflection on what Epilepsy can do to a life. As a person starts to get to know their difference, they apologize for things they cannot control. It is hard to understand why change enters a life and it can be hard to find good reason for its existence. When a person sees people accepting, they are met with confusion. With shakes and unexpected falls, seizures become a frustration. As changes continue, understanding from other people cannot be accepted until they admit that Epilepsy is not their fault. Apologies are not needed. Seizures are a challenge and acceptance is the tool for forgiveness. In life, try to accept, learn and enjoy.

Disability

Disability
Is that an inability?
No. It is a challenge
To live your life differently

It can be a scare
To people that are unaware
Give yourself knowledge
Disability becomes a dare

Be yourself the best
Acceptance will put fears to rest
Disability?
Conquer your Personal Life's Quest

This was a poem written to express how a person can feel having a disability. A person can meet others with a disability and choose to learn from them. Understanding helps a person to find acceptance and put fears to rest. Looking at a disability as a start to a different life is a good perspective to have. As a person gets to know their differences they are reminded of how each situation is confusion to uninformed people. When given knowledge people are more prepared to face the challenge. This is the reason why a person should inform strangers of their disability from the start. Work with everyone around you; help people to welcome their experience. An open and honest environment is the place to be ready to learn and welcome new friends.

Understanding Another

Understanding another
Is not an easy function
As hard as we try
We are met with confusion

As difficult as it is
We shouldn't stop trying
For when it is figured out
It can be electrifying

A gift to know another
Wonderful to have a new friend
Confusion will still be met
But gifts can last, and have no end

This is a reflection on friendship. Everyone meets new people, gets to know them and discovers new ways to learn. They work hard to know and understand their friends. As friendship grows they have confusion of their friends' ways. It can feel difficult but never stop trying. As they continue they get to know another that is different from their person. Every person we get to know brings us lessons to learn and experiences to value. In getting to know people around us we welcome what life has to offer.

Your Challenges

Your challenges can frighten you
Life lessons that enlighten you
Each lesson will help you to grow
Your acceptance helps you to know
Lessons are valuable and encourages
Don't listen to your fears, learn from your challenges

Differences cause you to wonder
Makes you feel you are asunder
Lessons help you to uncover
The self you're meant to discover
Try to enjoy and accept experiences
Respect the gifts given from your differences

This was a reflection of a time filled with Life Challenges. A person can get frightened of their challenges but when they allow life lessons in, they are enlightened. Every lesson is given to a person to help them grow and with acceptance, they start to know. When a person finds understanding of their lessons, they can be encouraged. Fears should never be held onto, it is best to remain open to learning.

Life lessons uncover many differences in a person. As differences get known, questions need answers. Accepting lessons leads a person to know who they are meant to be. To discover the self a person needs to accept and enjoy their experiences. Differences are part of each person.

We Face Many Changes

Though we can often feel left out
That is not what it's about
We each have a role that's separate
Even ones that don't feel definite

In life we face many changes
To our own single role
We each have to accept and rearrange
Even if difficulty takes a toll

Care from others can often confuse
We often feel a need to refuse
Acceptance will help us to grow closer to another
Helping to build true understanding from the other

This is a reflection of when changes in life trouble a person. People have to listen to warnings they are given. This causes them to be left out but remember that caution is not exclusion. Everyone has their own journey to travel, even when the path is not understood. These are times when changes occur. A person needs to accept and work with changes, even when it feels difficult to continue.

In these times a person is offered help from people that care and it can be confusing. Working on understanding change, a person often refuses help and pushes others away. Acceptance of themselves is the action that will help them understand the care that they are offered. In welcoming others closer they are admitting needed help and building true understanding from the other.

Acceptance of Difference

Be open to express
Others don't know you well
Difference, share with all
Not a value that makes you small

Acceptance of difference
And the gifts it has to offer
The many things it gives
And the values found as one lives

Don't fear lessons given
Accept good in your difference
Get to know gifts that's you
Share it with others, keep it true

This is a reflection on how important it is for a person to accept their difference. Difference makes a person into their own person. Share with others and understanding is found. Lessons are learned and there is no need to have fears. See the good in your difference and help others to know you, too.

In Different Ways to Us It Appears

In different ways to us it appears
But don't be threatened by your fears
We have to use the power we own
Even when we are feeling very alone

Enjoy the experience that is for you
Even if it is shared by very few
Live your life and be complete
Accept your challenges but don't delete

A wonderful tool it can be to use
Not a gift for you to abuse
Applied to the best of your ability
It will become a personal utility

This poem is a reflection on how to accept new lessons. Different life lessons will appear and cause one to feel afraid but, as you want to learn and get to know yourself, fears cannot be allowed to be a threat. Lessons helps you realize that you are able when you use the abilities you have.

Experiences come in many ways. They can be hard and confusing and they can also be joyous and rewarding. We should always try to enjoy the experience meant for our person. We may not be able to go to and receive understanding but to experience is to live. To find our joys we need to accept our new lessons and let them be great tools for us to refer.

Chances

Chances come in many forms,
Even in the darkest storm.
It matters how you perceive it,
In all forms you shall receive it.

Positive thought, a light
Of which makes all darkness bright.
Helps you look towards tomorrow
And leave behind you all sorrows.

Chances seen are a great gift.
For your spirit they will lift.
It is something to appreciate,
They are the gifts that motivates.

These are words about perception, an important tool in one's life. Sometimes a chance is presented to a person but when viewed as a curse, the value of the chance is reduced. Positive thought helps one to have hope and survive hardships. It brightens the darkness, encourages you to look ahead and helps you leave sadness behind. When chances are recognized it gives one's spirit a lift. Appreciate your thoughts, they are there to motivate and encourage you. As long as you want the light it will come back after lessons are learned.

Opportunity Comes in Many Forms

Opportunity comes in many forms
With a proper gift for the person
In various packages it is provided
And up to the person to fairly divide it

We may run into challenges
Have difficulties to overcome
But success is still a reward
A good goal to work towards

Have faith in your journey
Accept the rewards you are given
Give your work appreciation
And provide yourself some recognition

This poem is a reflection on times when opportunity enters a life. As a person looks at the gifts of life, they come in different packages and it is up to the person to recognize them. Having faith in their journey they experience and accept rewards meant for their person. It is important to have self-confidence, to know who they are and work towards what they want.

Never forget to give yourself the appreciation that you deserve.

Individuals

Hard to Exist

Hard to exist, when not able
Living normally, a fable
Understanding not really found
Medical issues, to me bound
Common methods of life, I find hard to resist
Odd differences can make it hard to exist

I am wishing to not be me
If it came true, there'd be a fee
The gifts I own would not be there
My life would not feel blessed and fair
Doubts and fears, in my mind, constantly need squishing
Happiness with my own person, I am wishing

It can be hard to continue when difficulties are haunting the days. To live 'normally' becomes a dream that requires work. A person searches for understanding and may feel it is not there. Don't blame any medical issues. Remember, understanding can still be found.

Common lessons of life are there to experience but differences make it hard to continue. A person can wish to be someone else but have to be aware that valued gifts are lost if that wish came true. To not be who you are is to face a different set of troubles. This is a reminder to remain your own person and enjoy your gifts. Stop giving doubts and fears any credit. Happiness with who you are is a life goal that has much worth.

A Challenge to Your Person

A challenge to your person
Not an embarrassment
A lesson for you to learn
Not a time for you to fear

Get to know your person
Focus on your goals
Don't choose to give up
Find your strength and keep going

Stay open to the lessons
Use different perspectives
Find acceptance
To all gifts you are offered

There are times when a person finds comfort and then meets a challenge. Without understanding it feels like an embarrassment, not a feeling to believe in. A person feels a fear and questions what is happening. Take a time out to get to know your person. Give yourself a chance and find your purpose. Giving up is not wanted. Work for your strength, focus on a goal and keep going in the direction you desire. As lessons get introduced try to be open to them. The use of different perspectives allows a person to experience. In hard times it is important to be accepting and your life will be what it was meant to be.

Be Who You Want To Be

We each should set a goal
To which we want to strive
We need to enjoy its blessings
When it finally arrives

Our goals can often vary
Change as life progresses
Confusion and questions are met
As we aim for successes

Never stay in question
Or choose anger in your journey
Have and keep determination
Continue your steps forward and be who you want to be

This poem was written as a summary of the one most important thing a person should do for their life, set goals to work towards. As a person strives for their goals, they encounter a variety of experiences that are blessings that help make the journey towards their goals more rewarding.

As life progresses, a person is met with many changes that can cause their goals to get altered. They often get confused and have questions to answer but, when they keep an open mind and continue to aim for their goals, success is a possibility. Never allow your person to remain in question or be angered by the changes you are given, those are ways that will halt your progress. In times of doubt or question, it is best to have determination and keep it. Focusing on your wanted goal is a great way to keep moving forward and allowing yourself to be the person you want to be.

The Person You Were Meant To Be

Try to become the person you were meant to be
Learn from others but keep your originality
We should never want to be like another completely
That creates an unoriginal person to be

We have moments of hardship and get confused
But giving up can cause us to lose
Learn from all the decisions you make
Even the ones that have been mistakes

There are many options to be the way you should
The option to remain your person is very good
Believe in the person that you are
Do your best and you will go far

E very person is an original person for the world. They learn from others and wish to be others but they should always work with the person they were meant to be. When faced with difficulties they wish to stop trying but giving up turns away the opportunities provided.

A decision can be a mistake but try to learn from all decisions. Errors in life are lessons. Always make an effort to believe in your efforts. Doing your best you will go far and become the success you were meant to be.

Moments of Difference

Moments of difference
For times of growth and discovery
To build personal acceptance
And provide personal recovery

It can feel like an impossibility
Though up to us to have access
It is a personal responsibility
To know our desired success

Use determination
To continue and to grow
Personal appreciation
Make differences great to show

This poem is a reflection on the meaning of being different. At times when differences overwhelm, causing one to feel unable, start to face differences and what it means for life. These are the moments to rediscover your person and what you want. Determination is a valuable tool to help you to continue, grow and truly know what you need. The other valuable tool is personal appreciation. As much as you want to work for others, it is important to recognize your own actions. Through personal appreciation you are giving yourself credit for your work and becoming an example that will not be feared by others.

Your Wanted Focus

Allow yourself to find a focus
And allow yourself to enjoy
Appreciate all things given
Observe it all and stay striven

It's up to you to know what's wanted
And it's up to you to accept
Have lessons help your wanted focus
And in all that happens, have respect

No need to worry or judge your person
You are one with your own purpose
Allow discovery to help lead your way
And on your wanted focus, continue to stay

T his was inspired at a time when differences were needed to be accepted. At first there was a fear but then a reminder of how much is lost if acceptance is not found. In times of question there is no need to worry or judge our person. We have to remember that we have a purpose and we work to find it. Small discoveries will help us on our way and it is up to our person to stay focused. This reminder is an encouragement, it lets one know that they are allowed to find their goals to focus on and enjoy.

Self - Acceptance

Brand new moments filled with surprise
Times of our lives we should revise
Not a sign that we are all wrong
Just a time to try and be strong
A time to experience new life elements
To learn and grow with the use of brand new moments

Self-acceptance, a wanted key
Helps us know what we're meant to be
Discovery welcomes what's new
Helps us to know what can be true
We often look to others for some alliance
But it's always best to start with self-acceptance

This poem was a small review on what life can be and a quality to maintain to help us to be the best we can be. Every life is filled with brand new moments that are surprises. Those are the times to take in and make any changes we need to make to continue our journey. It can often cause us to question but we must remain strong to experience our life. We ask others, for assistance, but answers are not fully there until we are able to accept our person and know our person. When life is experienced, we are provided the opportunity to grow as a person.

At Times When Things Seem So Distant

At times when things seem so distant
Confidence disappears in an instant
Questions begin to arise
Questions wondering why you're alive

Although you may not be a star
Always believe in who you are
For you are an original
And your life is continual

There's a reason why you were put here
Though it may not be how it appears
Its purpose will come at its own time
And with you, it will align

E ach person has a time when things are out of reach. When things seem at a distance, they feel insecure and wonder of their existence. They need to remember; they are not known in the entire world and it is their responsibility to believe in their person. They do not fit in but that has everything to do with being different. Times filled with doubts are the times for self-discovery and growth.

When we discover what to follow, we get to know our purpose, find answers and know why we are here. We are more patient for things to align with our person.

Approval from the Main Crowd

Work towards your goals
With intentions that are whole
No need to impress
To become a 'success'

For what do you wish to do?
What results to come true?
As long as intents are good
Things will become what it should

This was inspired by the lesson of accepting the self. Thoughts that something is wrong when we are different from the main crowd are not thoughts to have. There is no need to be so scared, we just need to discover our goals and be sure that the intentions are proper.

We fear to believe that we are good because we want approval from others. Remember: Don't impress for success. As goals are set, find what you truly wish to do. Get to know the results you want, work with proper intentions, and then have your goals succeed.

Motivation

Motivation,
Incentive for action
Valuable reasons
To promote reaction

Found from within
Towards a wanted purpose
Distribute it around
Have it be continuous

Keep strong belief
In your goals desired
Focus on your reason
Stay driven and motivated

M otivation gives a person reason to start moving towards their goals. As a person places their actions in motion, they start to see results they want. It can be inspired by another but, until they find it, their goals remain in place. With a goal, they have a purpose. It is theirs but still best to share with others.

It is a responsibility to focus on the goals made. Within a journey, reasons will be altered but up to a person to know what they want. When they know what they want they have to work towards it and, with motivation, they will accomplish their goals.

Keep on Trying, Don't Give Up

There's no need to look so sad
There's no need to stay so mad
Everyone will have some change
Need a time to rearrange

Never choose to believe doubt
Never choose to trust in fear
Everyone has Time for Growth
Choose to get to know yourself

It takes time to understand
It takes time to experience
Everyone takes their own road
Time's needed to learn and grow

Keep on going, don't look back
Keep on your desired track
Everyone knows what they want
Keep on trying, don't give up.

This was a poem inspired at a time when life was filled with change. As changes started to occur, new doubts and fears awakened, causing feelings of sadness and anger. It had to be admitted, everyone goes through change in their life and those are the times they need to rearrange their person. Trusting their fears causes them to stop and stay in their place. As they hear their doubts and fears they are being introduced to a time for Personal Growth. This becomes a time to find some courage and get to know their true person.

As we enter our journey we realize that time is needed for us to be able to experience new things and find understanding in the experience. Every single person has their own road because we all learn differently and we all have experience differently. We ask others for help and we listen to the advice from others but we all need our own time to learn and grow.

As hardships are encountered you need to keep on going and let go of past experiences. Use your past as a guider but when you hold on to it you prevent new lessons from entering. As a person opens themselves up to new experiences they allow themselves to remain on their desired track. It can introduce itself as a complete difference but with acceptance they will start to understand its purpose.

Keep On Going

Keep on going at your own pace
Keep in mind: It is not a race
This is a journey meant for you
Not meant for many, just for you
Don't stop because you feel progress is not showing
Maintain your hard work and efforts, keep on going

Answers will come at their own time
And when ready, with you align
Causing you a shock or surprise
Giving a help to realize
The current gifts in your life add up to a sum
And when the hard questions arise, answers will come

This is a reflection on times when differences are hard to accept. A person needs to pay attention to their own abilities, stop trying to be someone else. Hard work means a lot, even when we do not know from others. Efforts, working slowly, take us to where we want to be. Answers come at their own time and show us that small progress sums up to a great accomplishment.

Love

A New Adventure

A new adventure
For new people I meet
To see a seizure
When I have a seat

They look in question
And often as why
Looks of confusion
As they see me try

It happens to inform
Give new lessons to learn
It helps thoughts to be reformed
Have purpose and return

This poem was inspired by loving people in this world. Looks of question can be a worry but it is a help to the world to live openly. Other people with problems can learn from what is shared. A person, when being open, learns that other people are scared when not informed. With proper information fears can be erased and courage can be discovered. Everybody can fear the unknown but, with knowledge, everybody will be secure and learn.

Love Yourself

Fear of your person
Allows others to follow, too
It gives permission
To not love you as you

Accept your situation
Though shared by very few
Be open to all
Allow you to be you

Keep your originality
Be the only one that's you
Share your speciality
Love yourself for being you

This was a reflection on why it is important to love yourself. As a person with epilepsy looks around for help they have to know what they want. Love for your person comes first from yourself. As this lesson is accepted the truth in it will be seen. When a person chooses to be scared of epilepsy, others will also be scared. Epilepsy can appear like a hardship shared by very few but when having acceptance, it turns into an original quality. It truly is up to a person to love their person. When one shares their person they are contributing to the world.

Reactions May Differ

It is not the result that matter most
It is the intention that counts
Reactions may differ
But it is the good that amounts

Stop your focus on other people
And try to remember you
You are of importance as well
Your care will come first from you

You need to accept from others
Their given love and care
In thinking of yourself
You share and are fair

This poem is a reflection for a person facing new differences. When difficulties become more real, a person can feel guilty and believe that they are wrong. They forget the good that they do and believe that others would be angered the same way they are. They have to remember that they are a person of different needs. When asking for help they will not always meet the reactions expected. A person will have to do their best to get the help needed. They cannot focus on thoughts they think others have, they have to remember why help is needed. Thinking of the self is still giving to others. When help is offered accept openly without worries. The best way for a person to be cared for is by accepting offered help and remembering their person.

Don't worry about
how you look

Don't worry about how you look
For you have a lot to handle
Others don't have a clue
All because they are not you

It is altered every day
Making it all brand new
It causes question and wonder
Encourages lesson and growth

Don't choose to doubt
As it prevents and slows
Remember your efforts
And acknowledge what it shows

This is a reflection on the worries people have about they appear to others. A person wonders how they are viewed because they don't like what they see. They have to remain calm and admit that thoughts from others are not a main concern. Others, because they are different, cannot know what is going on. As hard as one tries to explain what is going on, others cannot know unless they are that person.

Every day is a new day filled with alterations. They cause question and wonder, ways that encourages a person to welcome lessons and personal growth. When doubt is chosen to be considered, it prevents things and slows it down. In choosing to continue and not allow doubts to prevent, people are blessed to see how efforts contribute to a person. Not seen by all but a responsibility for a person to acknowledge and welcome it.

Belief in Me

To offer belief in me
Shows that they care
However, the strength of their belief
Is quite a scare

Acceptance of their care
Is a responsibility
For a person who can and cannot
A person with changing abilities

Changes happen
Constantly day to day
Expecting others to know
Can never be the way

Acceptance has to come from the self
Though wished for from friends and family
It's important to maintain my given beliefs
I need to love and care for the person that is me

This poem is a reflection on how belief for a person can be misunderstood. When a person's life is overwhelming they wonder why others are not bothered. As others show their faith, it is mistaken that beliefs will not be lived up to. The idea of acceptance feels like a responsibility when help is needed.

A person has to remember that changes happen and others cannot be expected to know. Acceptance of a person comes first from the self. As much as one needs care, it is up to them to know their needs and be the first to care. Without communicating how and what is needed others cannot provide. Changing abilities are given to help one discover their person. Belief from others proves there is love in the world, even when a person feels alone on their journey.

A Table That Seats Many

There are many things to bring
To a table that seats many
Qualities, gifts and examples
That can be picked up by any

The table may seat strangers
You may not know what is needed
But use your gifts to give and offer
Your limits: Try to exceed it

Try to always do your best
Remember your abilities
Never allow limits to frighten
Have belief, keep tranquility

We all have much to offer
A help to the many we meet
Never allow questions to cause doubt
Have faith, choose to stay in your seat

This is a reflection for a person finding their place in life. An important perspective to consider, 'Every single person has a different gift to add to a table.' Having a difference causes a person to question their place. They need to look at the good they do offer. Challenges are for rediscovery. There are times when a person feels their limits have been met but it is always best to exceed the limits and try new possibilities. It is a gift to have belief in our person. It is also a gift to the people around us to view our abilities and beliefs, an inspiration for them to try as well.

Intentions Consists Great Value

Intentions consists great value
To the meaning of our actions
Though we cannot expect
Our wanted reactions

We search for understanding
Though it is not always found
We are met with confusion
Though intentions remain sound

We have to believe in our person
Maintain consistent intentions
Stay true to the desired results
Continue intended communications

There are so many different ways for people to act but they have to understand their intentions. When understanding is not found from others, don't allow it to lead to improper assumptions. People should not be angered or alter their intentions. It is best to hold onto the goal and continue. Understanding cannot be found when someone is encountering a personal journey. Every person travels differently and will accept their help at their own time.

Communication

Communication can be a gift
To inform, educate and even prevent
Reactions can be a big surprise
Often causing unwanted worries to relent

It is good to share your person
To be open and honest
Openness of your character
A key to put worries to rest

We are all here for a reason
Even if it is mysterious
Enjoy the life you are given
No need to only be serious

T his poem was inspired by communication. A person needs
inform others and not worry of troubles they had been
warned of. When a person communicates with others they are
met with a welcome to friendship. When you believe you are not
a scare, you are calmed and open. Talking with others helps to
bring understanding. Openness makes a person feel wanted and
included. We start as strangers and sharing helps everyone be more
comfortable. Communication is a great gift for everyone.

A Situation Can Be Mistaken

A situation can be mistaken
Seen in a different way
Filled with various lessons
To help make up your day

It can often appear to be all wrong
No good for the opportunity
But often it's possibly misread
It is actually the way it should be

Stop reading into every life situation
And let them take their course
You may not currently want it right now
But one day it may be a good source

New experiences can confuse and cause question. The moment introduces itself and a person is required to change their ways. As others watch, they can mistake the changes in that person. Why would a person who looks cared for need care? What is their purpose?

When we are misread we feel that we are wrong. When we view the situation with an open mind we start to see that it is an experience to learn. It is best to not make up our answers and let the situation take its course. We know that hardship is not wanted but it is a lesson for another time. Mistakes can be the lesson meant for growth.

When We Want To Be Included

There's a time when we want to be included
But we have to remember why we are excluded
It is not for reasons that are unfair
The reasons are because others care

Differences can often be hard to receive
But not a personal quality for us to deceive
We need to learn and get to know its affects
Treat it with kindness and respect

It is not given to us to disable or prevent
It is not something for us to resent
It is a challenge to help us learn and grow
It can become a gift for us to show

Have positivity, don't be sad
Keep an open mind, don't be mad
Despite differences, enjoy your place
Try to stay happy and keep a smile on your face

When people watch out for a person with epilepsy, it can be mistaken as exclusion. The person with epilepsy wishes for understanding but is unable to find acceptance of the self. They need a time out, look at their person and review everything. It is best for them to be open to their difference and consider alternate perspectives. This allows the person to grow and their difference can become a tool.

With a positive outlook a person experiences more happiness and they start to enjoy what they have. Differences are challenging but with belief anything can be accomplished. With a smile people will want to care and not be afraid.